Searchlight
BOOKS™

Cutting-Edge STEM

Cutting-Edge
Artificial Intelligence

Anna Leigh

D1716400

Lerner Publications ◆ Minneapolis

For the Murchie boys

Lerner Publications Company
A division of Lerner Publishing Group, Inc.
241 First Avenue North
Minneapolis, MN 55401 USA

For reading levels and more information, look up this title
at www.lernerbooks.com.

Main body text set in Adrianna Regular 14/20.
Typeface provided by Chank.

Library of Congress Cataloging-in-Publication Data

Names: Leigh, Anna, author.
Title: Cutting-edge artificial intelligence / Anna Leigh.
Description: Minneapolis : Lerner Publications, [2019] | Series: Searchlight books.
   Cutting-edge stem | Includes bibliographical references and index. | Audience:
   Ages 8–11. | Audience: Grades 4 to 6.
Identifiers: LCCN 2018006136 (print) | LCCN 2018013573
   (ebook) | ISBN 9781541525368 (eb pdf) | ISBN 9781541523487 (lb : alk. paper) |
   ISBN 9781541527737 (pb : alk. paper)
Subjects: LCSH: Artificial intelligence—Juvenile literature. | Automation—Juvenile
   literature.
Classification: LCC TA347.A78 (ebook) | LCC TA347.A78 L45 2019 (print) |
   DDC 006.3—dc23

LC record available at https://lccn.loc.gov/2018006136

Manufactured in the United States of America
1-44421-34680-5/3/2018

Contents

Chapter 1

WHAT IS ARTIFICIAL INTELLIGENCE?

Lee Sedol stared down at a wooden game board covered in black and white stones. He was one of the best players in the world of an ancient Chinese game called Go. But he had just lost the game to a computer program called AlphaGo.

Go is the oldest board game that people still play. It started in China more than twenty-five hundred years ago.

Lee Sedol (*right*) studies the Go board. The man on the left is placing a stone on the board for AlphaGo.

AlphaGo is an artificial intelligence (AI) program. AI allows a computer to learn, make decisions, and react as humans do. AI programs can learn to process information on their own. Human programmers build computers with AI in different ways.

Machine Learning

How do you tell a dog from a cat? When you see a dog, you can instantly tell what kind of animal it is because you have seen dogs before. You see the shape of its ears, its nose, and its tail, and you know that you are looking at a dog.

Cats and dogs share many features, such as ears and noses. You can tell a cat from a dog because of the differences in those features.

Programmers create AI that can learn.
That way the AI can react to situations
programmers can't predict.

AI programs work the same way. It would be very complicated for a programmer to write code with all the steps for recognizing dogs. Instead, programmers use machine learning so the computer can teach itself the differences between dogs and other animals.

A programmer using machine learning might show an AI thousands of images of dogs. The AI analyzes and compares the images. Later, if the computer sees a new picture of a dog, the AI will recognize it.

Coding Spotlight

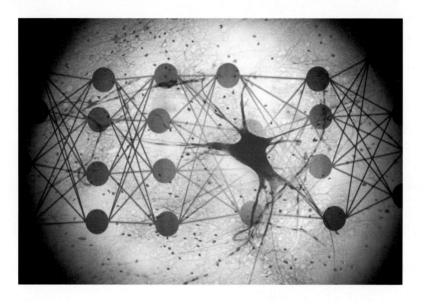

A neural network is an AI structure that works like the human brain. The human brain contains cells called neurons that connect to one another to send signals through the brain. An AI neural network uses layers of electronic neurons. The first layer analyzes simple pieces of an image, sound, or text. Then this layer passes information to the next layer, which analyzes different parts. This process continues until the program understands the whole image or sound.

AlphaGo's programmers used machine learning to teach it to play Go. The programmers showed the computer many games of Go. AlphaGo learned the moves in these games. Then it began playing games against itself to practice and learn new moves. The computer built up a database of knowledge about the game. While playing Go, the computer could use its database to consider moves and choose the best one.

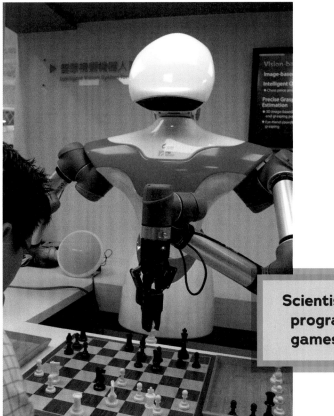

Scientists have taught AI programs to play many games, including chess.

Chapter 2

EVERYDAY AI

AI is quickly becoming a part of everyday life. Computers can recognize voices and faces. They can sort through information on websites. Many people use AI in their homes and at work. You may use AI without even realizing it!

AI programs can learn to recognize your voice.

A FAMILY HAS FUN WITH ECHO,
A DEVICE THAT CONNECTS TO ALEXA, AMAZON'S
VOICE-CONTROLLED VIRTUAL ASSISTANT.

▼

Intelligent Home

One morning while getting ready for school, you can't decide if you should wear a T-shirt or a sweater. You call out, "What's the weather like today?" A person doesn't answer. Instead, you hear an artificial voice say, "It's warm and sunny outside." You grab a T-shirt to wear.

Amazon's Echo can help you run other devices and track your schedule. Or you can just have a conversation with it.

Many people use virtual assistants. These programs may be in computers or smartphones. They may be in speakers or other devices that connect to the internet. Virtual assistants respond to voice commands. You can ask the assistant for information such as the weather forecast, or you can ask it to play music or turn on your lights. When you speak to the assistant, it analyzes the tone and patterns of your voice to understand your question. Then it responds by accessing information from the internet or by sending signals to apps or other devices.

AI in Action

Companies are working on self-driving cars. Many of these vehicles use AI technology. The cars need to analyze the world around them to know where to go, what other nearby vehicles are doing, and when to stop. Programmers can't teach the car how to act in every situation it might encounter. So the cars use AI to make decisions about how to drive on a new road and avoid accidents.

WHEN YOU BUY SOMETHING ONLINE, AI MIGHT NOTICE THE PURCHASE AND SEND YOU ADS FOR SIMILAR PRODUCTS.

Internet Intelligence

People might also use AI when they shop. You may buy a book from a website. The next time you visit that website, it suggests other books for you to buy. The website chooses them by accessing information online about books that are similar to the book you bought. Television and movie streaming services use similar technology to recommend new shows and movies for you to watch.

Social media uses AI too. When you post a photo on social media, the AI program compares the photo to other images of you and your friends. It looks at face shapes, facial features, and hair color to figure out who is in the photo. A program might recognize that you often watch funny videos about cats and show you lots of cat videos. It might see that you often post about football and show you more articles about football. The program tracks your activity to figure out what you want to see.

If you like fun cat photos like this one, online AI programs will make sure that you see plenty of them on the internet.

Chapter 3

AI AT WORK

AI can do a lot more than play games and help you shop. It can be incredibly useful in professional settings. The ability to quickly sort and analyze lots of information is very important in some jobs.

AI can help one person do work that would take many people to accomplish without AI.

Legal arguments are often based on the outcomes of previous cases. AI can help lawyers sort through many previous legal cases to find one that helps their argument.

Lawyers help people and companies in legal situations. Lawyers use information about history, laws, and much more to make arguments to win a legal case. It can take months for people to find the right information. But an AI program can find information much more quickly. It can sort through thousands of legal cases and compare their arguments and outcomes. Then the lawyer knows which arguments are likely to win the case.

Science Fact or Science Fiction?

AI can make up stories.

This is true—sort of!

Some news groups have begun using AI programs to write simple stories such as sports reports. One team of researchers created a program to write horror stories. But AI writing programs need a lot of help from humans. They need examples of previously written stories to know how to write the next line of a horror story or understand the style of a sports report.

As AI programs get better at writing stories, newsrooms like this one may not need as many people to function.

During a medical emergency, doctors need to find health problems quickly using X-rays, and AI programs can help.

Doctors use AI too. An X-ray machine creates pictures of the inside of a person's body. A doctor can look at an X-ray image to find a broken bone or other problems. But a human doctor might not notice a very small tumor or a cracked bone in an X-ray. AI can quickly compare many different X-rays of the same body parts. Because it can compare so many samples, it is more likely to find a tiny problem in an X-ray.

Different medical treatments have different effects on cancer cells. AI can help doctors compare treatments.

AI can also help doctors treat diseases such as cancer. An AI program can analyze a patient's condition and access research, treatment options, and information about other patients from all around the world. It would take a doctor a long time to sort through all of this information. The program can quickly determine the best treatment for the patient.

School Days

Teachers can use AI as well. Not every student learns in the same way. But teachers often don't have enough time to work with every student one-on-one. So teachers can use AI programs to track how well students are learning or where they are making mistakes. Then the teacher can figure out how to help each student learn more easily.

AI progams can save teachers time by helping to monitor students' progress.

Chapter 4

AI FOR THE FUTURE

Many people are concerned about AI's future. They think that computers could one day become smarter than people. If that happens, computers might begin doing things we don't want them to do. Some people think AI will one day become dangerous.

In the movie *I, Robot*, starring Will Smith, robots with AI pose a threat to humanity.

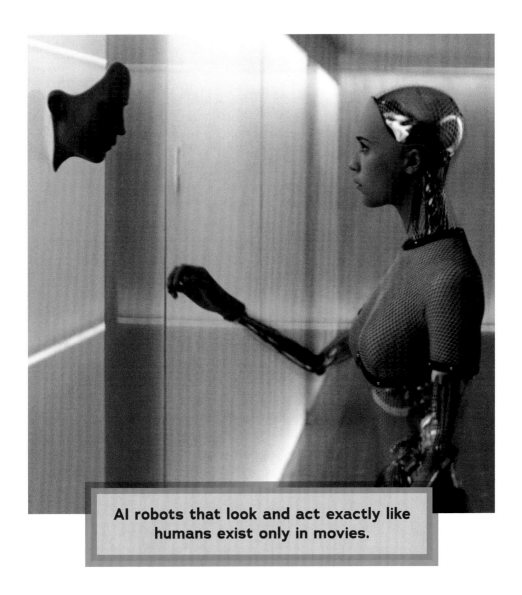

AI robots that look and act exactly like humans exist only in movies.

Lots of books, movies, and TV shows feature AI. Often in these stories, AI robots look a lot like humans. Humans work with the robots and even become friends with them. One day we might have AI robots like these.

Scientists are working on robots
that can express human emotions.
This robot's face and arms are
expressing surprise.

These kinds of robots use something called general
AI. With this kind of AI, robots would think, act, and
react on their own. They would have conversations and
show emotions just like a human. It might be difficult to
tell the difference between a human and a robot. But
programmers have not been able to perfect general
AI yet.

Instead, we have narrow AI. This kind of AI is designed to do specific tasks really well. It can't learn to do tasks that it hasn't been designed to learn. A Go-playing AI can't learn to play chess on its own. AI that helps a lawyer can't drive a car. Researchers think it will be many years before we can program general AI that is creative, that can change its mind, and that can think and act like a human.

Most robots with AI focus on specific tasks. This robot is making a pizza.

Science Fact or Science Fiction?

AI can create other AI.

Yes, this is true!

Google created an AI program called AutoML. It can create its own AI. An AI created by AutoML was actually better at recognizing objects in images than an AI that humans created. Even people untrained in machine learning and deep neural networks can create AIs using AutoML. Such programs will allow AI to become more common, and with more use, AI will develop more quickly and become more intelligent.

Some AI programs learn to recognize images of people and other objects.

AI Can Help

Many people think AI will make humans smarter, more creative, and better at doing their jobs. Some Go players have changed the way they play the game because they learned new moves from AlphaGo. Maybe computers can teach humans other skills too. AI could help humans cure cancer, end wars, and protect the environment.

AI could help keep Earth clean. This AI robot is collecting trash from a harbor near France.

AI technology is getting better every day. Nobody knows what the future of AI will look like. But most people agree that AI will someday be incredibly important.

Some people feel more comfortable communicating with objects such as robots than with other people. Researchers are developing this AI robot to communicate with people who have autism.

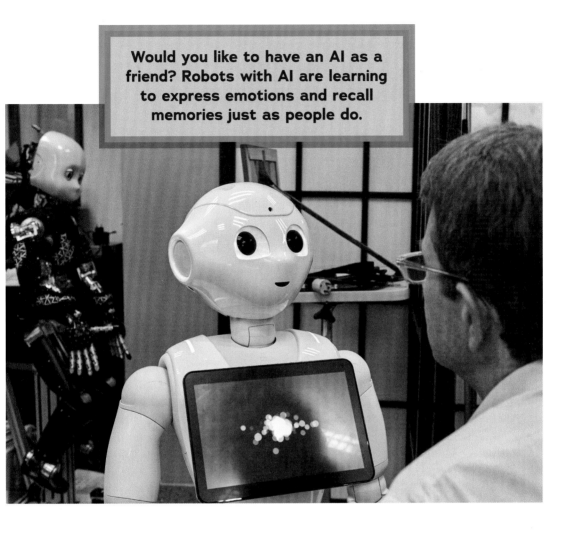

Would you like to have an AI as a friend? Robots with AI are learning to express emotions and recall memories just as people do.

Maybe one day you'll make the next breakthrough in AI. Or maybe you'll work next to a supersmart AI robot on a project no one has even dreamed of yet!

Glossary

analyze: to study closely and carefully

code: instructions that make up a computer program

database: a collection of information that is organized and stored on a computer

professional: related to a specific job

program: instructions for a computer to follow to complete a task

programmer: someone who creates computer programs

track: to follow or watch the path of someone

virtual: existing on computers or the internet

Learn More about Artificial Intelligence

Books

Gregory, Josh. *Artificial Intelligence*. Ann Arbor, MI: Cherry Lake, 2017. Learn more about the history, present, and future of artificial intelligence.

Kenney, Karen Latchana. *Cutting-Edge Robotics*. Minneapolis: Lerner Publications, 2019. Read all about robots, including some that look like humans and use AI.

Lindeen, Mary. *Humanoid Robots*. Minneapolis: Lerner Publications, 2018. Learn about humanoid robots with AI, how they're made, and what they might look like in the future.

Websites

Robots for Kids
http://www.sciencekids.co.nz/robots.html
Check out games, projects, videos, and more about robots and artificial intelligence.

Self-Driving Cars
http://mocomi.com/self-driving-cars
Read more about one cool way AI technology is being used.

What Is Artificial Intelligence?
https://www.kidscodecs.com/what-is-artificial-intelligence
Learn more about AI and its uses.

Index

Photo Acknowledgments

Image credits: kc look/Shutterstock.com, p. 4; Google/Getty Images, p. 5; Gladskikh Tatiana/ Shutterstock.com, p. 6; Cameron Spencer/Getty Images, p. 7; jxfzsy/iStock/Getty Images, p. 8; SAM YEH/AFP/Getty Images, p. 9; panuwat phimpha/Shutterstock.com, p. 10; Bill O'Leary/The Washington Post/Getty Images, p. 11; Zapp2Photo/Shutterstock.com, pp. 12, 26; Kim Kulish/Corbis/Getty Images, p. 13; Rawpixel.com/Shutterstock.com, p. 14; The Len/ Shutterstock.com, p. 15; GaudiLab/Shutterstock.com, p. 16; Amnaj Khetsamtip/Shutterstock. com, p. 17; Jonathan Torgovnik/Getty Images, p. 18; visivastudio/Shutterstock.com, p. 19; STEVE GSCHMEISSNER/SCIENCE PHOTO LIBRARY/Getty Images, p. 20; Monkey Business Images/Shutterstock.com, p. 21; 20th Century Fox Film Corp/Courtesy Everett Collection, p. 22; © A24/Courtesy Everett Collection, p. 23; AP Photo/Koji Sasahara, p. 24; INGO WAGNER/AFP/Getty Images, p. 25; BORIS HORVAT/AFP/Getty Images, p. 27; BSIP/UIG/Getty Images, pp. 28, 29.

Cover: Ociacia/Shutterstock.com.